F

Through Open Windows of Jerusalem

Even Birds Sing During Storms

Kendra Turner

"Life altering decisions are made from fear or faith, and the foundation of one will crumble."

FIRST WORDS
Atlanta, Georgia

The author of this book does not dispense
medical advice or prescribe the use of any
technique as a form of treatment for physical,
emotional, or medical problems without the
advice of a physician, either directly or
indirectly. The intent of the author is only to
offer information of a general nature to help
you in your quest for emotional and spiritual
well-being. In the event you use any of the
information in this book for yourself, the

author and the publisher assume no responsibility for your actions."

Paperback ISBN - 10: 0-9702940-2-6
ISBN -13: 978-0-9702940-2-9

Printed in the United States of America

www.kendraturner.com

Contents

for James and my mother

Through Open Windows of Jerusalem
Even Birds Sing During Storms

Author's Note

When you read *Through Open Windows of Jerusalem: Even Birds Sing During Storms*, may you experience joy, love, and inspiration—I desire that your joy radiates beyond what you imagine, and that windows of opportunities open for you and through you, enabling you to create opportunities for others. Poetry enthralls the imagination and soul of the reader, and God enriches an open heart. The poetry, prose, and inspirational messages in *Through Open Windows of Jerusalem: Even Birds Sing During Storms* is purposefully designed without one identified religion for the book's foundation, which may stir theological debate regarding personal and spiritual beliefs. There is reason for debate based on your choice to make one, and a debate in which I freely choose to allow you to participate without me. Life is better than debating issues of a nugatory matter.

Using the analogy of maps, similar to my first self-published book *Sacrificing Isaac: Obedience Is Better Than Sacrifice*, there are references to God as a cartographer of life maps with an emphasis of following directions based on choice, even when your path to your fulfilled purpose is plotted, obstructed, and planned by other people, or situations. And, when you make a choice, people, or situations can influence you and steer you toward a different direction, ultimately getting you off your path, and a path where love is lost.

God is the cartographer who uses the spoken Word, which becomes the life energy written on our hearts through love. And, love is the pen that designs our life maps. Love is the pen that is the compass of our choices. One of God's greatest attributes is the freedom of choice, and the freedom to choose is based on love. When you allow a saboteur to be your guide, you can veer off your purposed path, and forget how to give and receive love. Be your own guide!

Through Open Windows of Jerusalem: Even Birds Sing During Storms is another map. It's filled with inspiration to trust God, and trusting God means you can trust God's directions through tunnels of tragedy and tunnels of victory. Discovering what you can do with a soul surrendered to trust, unfolds your destiny when you go through the tunnels. Remind yourself that it doesn't matter what's at the end of the tunnel, instead it matters how you come out!

A plethora of choices from a family tragedy inspired the book's title, and those choices were made by people; people who represented obstacles, and people who represented hope. The tragedy stemmed from watching a loved one become hurt, then begin to recover, then hurt again, until death deployed its final earthly decision, and faith ushered in hope of living beyond the physical realm. A family tragedy with continuous repercussions from the incident over a span of eleven years left imprints on lives, and faith in God remained the defining denominator—faith in beginnings and endings, faith in old, new, and renewed dreams, faith in opportunities, and faith in yourself. Faith is the ability to believe in what you're unable to see, because you know it anyway—it's that unexplained gut feeling of intuition, that thought of uncertain certainty, or the condition of acted confidence without thought. Christianity believes "Now faith is the substance of things hoped for, the evidence of things not seen" (Hebrews 11:1 New King James Version).

Notice the beginning word, *now*. There is no reference to waiting for things to happen, and no reference to the past or future tense of time; there is one succinct word of time, *now*. What better joy is there than knowing and experiencing that God doesn't intend for you to wait for opportunities, or for things to happen, and God doesn't intend for you try and make things happen. God is an action God, and God expects us to be action-oriented by faith.

Through Open Windows of Jerusalem: Even Birds Sing During Storms is a faith-filled inspiration book of intentional creation. The poetry, prose, and messages are created out of moments of life. Moments with explained and unexplainable outcomes that resulted in increased spiritual growth of the soul. Have you ever allowed your soul to experience moments of silence? Nature?

Nature provides a look into God's creative wonder that silences a chaotic soul and opens the core of your heart for God to usher in love. Open windows reveal a surrendered soul ready to explore and accept life, whereas, shut windows keep you arrested and prevent you from weathering a storm.

Untether your soul from fear, hurt, jealousy, anger, unforgiveness, and whatever keeps your windows closed. Pull back the curtains, the shades, and the blinds–clean your windows and journey *Through Open Windows of Jerusalem: Even Birds Sing During Storms.*

Photo by unknown

Lessons from Birth

1°

"You can purchase and bargain ordinary things, but there is nothing to bargain with a priceless life."

Calmed with a hidden fear, I sensed worry in my mother's voice. When the phone rang late that afternoon, she told me his heart stopped. His heart stopped? His heart stopped. James, a healthy, 240 pound, body-building, thirty-three year old man fully coded on the operating table. Stunned by the news of my brother's heart stopping, there came a brief flashback of emotions of my father's death in 1999.

The announcement jolted my thinking, but there were no negative thoughts. Instead, my faith blinded them. The faith I held when dealing with my father's death differed, but life's unexpected announcement of when death may occur became the commonality between my father and brother. This announcement unfolded two years after my father died, and I continued to grapple in disbelief. I thought I knew God two years earlier, and the years before, but this tragedy introduced a triumphant spirit of hope, faith, unity, and prayer. And, the adrenaline of tragedy hushed death a little longer.

Mother's Day

Soft whispers in my ear,
Gentle touches from your kiss,
Arms surrounded me in warmth,
I remember being your baby.
Seeing you age is beautiful,
Seeing you happy is magnificent,
Seeing you smile, laugh, and filled with joy is
seeing you blessed.

For my mother

Sibling Song

We counted one, two, or three,
We ran, jumped, and played *Hide and Go Seek.*
We built tents made from sheets and books,
We played cops and robbers, and you were the
crook.

In the evening, you yelled, "Get out of my
room!"
During the early dawn, you'd ignore me if I
woke you too soon.
Through evening to night, I'd thrived to get on
your nerves,
We agreed to give the other payback as earned
and deserved.

Climbing tall trees,
Getting stung by bees,
Filled with days of catching fire flies,
We disturbed a bird's nest to see the eggs, then
put them back to peacefully lie.   20

Familiar things to cherish, both right and wrong,
A welcomed joy of forgiveness with love,

When remembering the sibling song.

Seeds

There are seasons for planting and seasons for harvesting, but when is the season for choosing seeds? People who cultivate know seeds come in varieties and grow with specific conditions and in different soil.

Different seeds produced in different seasons yield different results–outcomes are never the same. The moment air fills our lungs we are introduced to the four seasons: spring, summer, winter, and fall. And, when the seasons change, the seeds change too.

The heart is the core of a person, and the core reserves the seed of the soul. The heart yields the personality, the attitude, and pure intentions. Take a moment and read the following verse from the Bible: "To everything there is a season, a time for every purpose under heaven" (Ecclesiastics 3:1).

A person's heart plants, and cultivates year round based on their personality, attitude, and intentions, and the outcomes which represent the harvest are never the same. The seeds grow where they are planted, and determine where people sow, but they don't determine when and where the harvest occurs. There are seeds that tend to become scattered and manage to find soil, and it grows. Whether it is a weed or such, it grows into something.

One seed can yield a bountiful harvest, or a meager one. A person can decide to share the harvest or keep it themselves. Sharing provides opportunities to keep planting and harvesting, and shared seeds are replanted in their own soil.

Seeds may resemble another seed, but yield a different harvest. Seeds grow in their own time and into their purposed outcome.

The hearts of people are seeds planted in their own soil, growing in their own purpose, and harvesting the intended outcomes.

Parental Praise

Parents are feet fitted for a right pair of shoes.

Never give up on parents who desire to learn, they're big kids in huge bodies.

A parent who lacks patience, is a parent who forgot that patience helped them.

A perfect parent doesn't exist, but there does exist a parent who takes time to relearn things that once forgotten.

Depending on your perspective, seeing relatives or yourself in your child is scary or joyous.

A parent's love has boundaries and no limits.

 You may have a life without children, and yet, you may end up being a parent to someone.

It's okay to cross the barriers and become a child again, but it's unacceptable to cross the boundaries and rob a child of their childhood.

Children are the best role models for hard knocks. When they fall, they look for help, and when no one responds, they get up and keep going.

We know of foster children and foster parents. We know adults adopt children, and children say, "I was adopted." What if children could adopt adults?

Thinking

The choice of competing against you is different from competing with you.

Competition exists not to prove worth, it's for the spirit to settle challenge in the soul.

People will stop laughing at the shortcomings of others, when they realize they have the same.

You tend to meet friends in strange places, and you tend to come across enemies in the common ones.

People who are uninterested in knowing you fear your true personality.

Everyone has a gift or talent, there are few who

take the risks to test it.

People who are unable to make eye contact, are people

who hide their soul.

When you're well-liked pay attention to the intentions of people.

Everyday people and everyday things go together with everyday.

You can can compare life to a game of basketball–you dribble to move around players, you pass the ball, or choose to take jump shots, three point shots, or even drive the baseline, and you may incur fouls that evoke free throws–your plays make a difference in the game.

You can can compare life to a game of baseball–Someone or something tries to strike you out, or someone is in the field trying to get you out. Your bat provides an outlook to determine getting on base, and when on base you choose how to run the bases. Will you take one base at a time, steal, or slide to get home?

Photo by Joey Thompson

Waiting Womb

2°

"No one can return to the womb or recall its surroundings–people who give birth can reminisce of the comfort and pain."

Over eleven years, my mother drove back and forth to Austin and Temple to visit James. There were situations when friends checked on James for her, helped with his laundry, or gave her a moment of rest. Her dedication to his care and well-being were relentless. Visits to James were expected and unannounced at varying and numerous times in the day, because she learned that many care providers gave the proper care when aware of a visitor.

She taught full-time, and maintained high work evaluations despite the frustrations at work. The change of supervisors, lack of support, and their unwittingly effort to try and force early retirement brought her no discouragement. Her inner strength endured the physical pain her body suffered from the toll of caring for my brother, but her spirit and faith in God remained her rock. God ordained her ministry when she became a mother, a full-time ministry of motherly love.

Watching James' recovery prompted countless hours of personal ministry. Despite his physical appearance to outer or peering eyes, James enjoyed peace and sensed confrontation. His presence evoked calm and hope, and that was the reason my mother gave her womb to him everyday.

Blessed Birth

Hey, little child! Can you count one, two, and
three?
Can you hold up ten fingers and toes for
everyone to see?

Hey, little child! Your skin is milky smooth,
You've traveled a distance to bring us the good
news.

The day you were born brought jubilee,
We praised and danced rather than drinking
tea.

We awaited your arrival and pondered every
second and hour,
We held no boundary of imagination of what
God could flower.

* * *

We have no words for the day filled with
overflowing joy,
We were blessed with a baby girl instead of a
boy.

Now that you're part of our entire world,
You may become mommy's shopping mate, but
you'll forever be daddy's little girl.

The Reason

When the doors of life appear impossible to
open,
And, pain has no next of kin,
Calvary's cross is the reminder,
That a grave is not the end.
Jesus died by the hands of those who defied
him,
Part of the plan to grab the keys from death's
hand,
A Master who spoke about returning,
Taking those that believe to the Promise Land.

A Mother's Heart

You were a seed planted in love,
Cherished, nourished,
A gift from above.
My womb you breathed,
My heart I gave,
Now you're an angel above the grave.

Where Is It?

Where's the sincerity, hope, trust, and love?
- It's in the lyrics of a hymn.
- It's in the fingers of a pianist.
- It's in the voice of a soloist.
- And, in the poem of a psalmist.
- It's in the living Word of God.
- It's in you.

Reflection

In the core of your womb I breathed,
Whole, new, fragile, and open to discover an
unknown world.

Your breasts sheltered assurance,
Nurtured warmth, food,
The fundamental nature of motherhood.

I am you.
You and I are the same,
One.

Wrapped in your arms, close to your bosom,
Shared stares offered refuge,
A haven of love,
I see a mirrored reflection.
Beauty of spirit,
Meekness and flare,
Ingredients from your breasts sustained me
when young.

Heart humbled and filled with compassion,
Fidelity, and hope,
A continued legacy of being,
You encompassed many roles.

Mother as sister,
Sister as friend,
Never an enemy of the soul's intent.

I am you.
You and I are the same.

Lord Provider Prayer

Provide the unselfishness of Able in order to offer the best.
Provide a friendship like Moses,
And, the fighting spirit of Joshua.
Provide a willingness to take risks like Rahab,
Birthed with covenant as Noah.
Provide the faith and obedience of Abraham,
And, the trumpet and word of Gideon.
Provide the humble heart of David,
Seared in the strength of Sampson.
Provide the respect and grace of Naomi,
And, the restored blessings of Ruth.
Provide the unknown and vast prosperity of Solomon,
Overflowing with the the favor of Esther.
Provide the inner, life-changing strength of Job,
With imparted wisdom and insight of Daniel.
Provide the yielded spirit of Mary,
Filled with the meekness of Mary Magdalene.
Provided the quietness of Salome,
A minister of silent reaching.
Provide the proclamation of John,

Immersed with the boldness of Paul.
Above all else,
Provide the true Spirit of Jesus in me.
Amen.

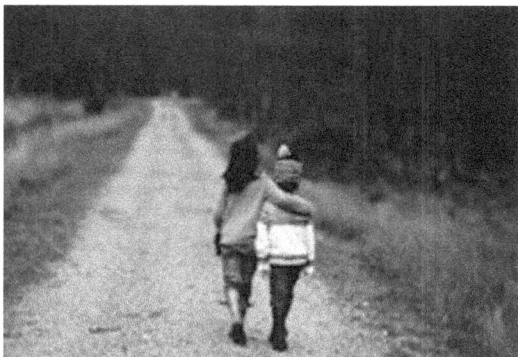

Photo by Annie Spratt

Timeless Talks

3°

"Age exists to end to soon or last to long."

James and I stood next to each other in silence. I gave no thought of this place, or if I had been here. This place felt familiar, but I recalled nothing of its dry, flat, mocha-cream ground. No trees, water, or brilliant-colored, landscaped sky filled this place, only a dark horizon. Though the horizon peeked of darkness, I encouraged James with words.

Words of an armored faith that urged him to wear the spiritual armor appearing near his feet. The armor God provided for a spiritual battle. James glanced at me unable to comprehend the meaning, but he picked up the armor knowing that he could rely on me to interpret, and I did. Intuitive and unspoken, I interpreted each piece of armor. I started with the breastplate of righteousness, and the helmet of salvation; then, I continued with girding his loins with truth to ensure his feet were prepared with the gospel. The final pieces included his cloak, and the shield of faith. Following my inner voice, I encouraged James to raise his shield of faith high, keep his sword of the Spirit ready, and direct him to never to drop them. I told him that if they became heavy for him, I would help him keep them lifted. James and I looked forward and there appeared a horse. Once more, using unspeakable instincts, I told James to watch and listen to the person on the white horse. The right hand of the person on the horse was raised, and signified waiting for command.

This had to be a dream, but I felt James' faith. And, when I did, I knew that in this moment, James could fight and defeat death. The both of us prepared for battle, but I had started fighting, the moment my mother called me.

Pumped with adrenaline and evoked with spiritual emotions is the only way to describe the flight to see my brother and comfort my mother. I have no memory of the details of my flight, or which gate, but I do remember focusing on participating in a spiritual fight that would either catapult my faith, or open an unaware spiritual avenue. When I packed for the flight, I imagined packing spiritual tools as in a movie instead of clothes. You know, the movies where the priest pack tools for an exorcism? Clearly, I had watched too much television, but that is how it felt and that became the plan.

A plan to test the Word of God. A plan to think and believe in the impossible. A plan to do the unimaginable, regardless of what people thought, or how they responded. A plan to ignore the doctors and rely totally on God; therefore, I needed a willing heart. A heart to trust God with the situation, and the outcome. And, family emergencies are the situations that tend to humble the heart. Love humbled my heart, and my brother's heart needed me.

I followed a strict, spiritual schedule, and demanded that certain protocols for my brother. Each morning, I started at seven o'clock to pray in the chapel and ate one meal a day. All meals were taken between five and seven o'clock in the evening. The evenings concluded sitting with my mother in the I.C.U for the hospitals last scheduled family visit. When the visit ended, my mother and I

44

retreated to our hospital room for the night, and I slept until midnight, and continued with prayer until seven the next morning. I repeated this process for days until James's health improved. The determination to test the Word of God became an obsession, and the obsession progressed when God proved true.

The next morning, after reciting God's Word and praying, I saw James and I standing next to each other again in our armor, and this time James and I were marching. During my prayers, I understood that I became the eyes and ears for my brother. When I stood praying knowing that my mind had elevated to an unfamiliar, spiritual trance than I had ever experienced, I would open my eyes when finished, and find that I had moved from one prayer position to another.

The hospital stay was lengthy, and out of all the moments that I prayed daily, no other person prayed in the chapel. I knew God saved that place for James and me.

Grandmother's Gift

her love is innocent and endearing
moments are timeless treasures
seeds of her thoughts are continually
blossoming
sheltering life
simple, fragile, and strong,
unwithered by outward winds
a heart that is irreplaceable
uplifted through love
a relationship entwined with trust
agape love of a grandmother's gift.

Grandfather's Eyes

His skin resembled that of a prune with hair
silver and gray, and he stood elevated with his
short stature. His heart made him a giant.
Grandfather's eyes.

Walking into a silent room, laughter would
erupted in his presence. One spoken word
could break the silence and evoke joy.
Grandfather's eyes.

Rested on a book at least seven inches thick
were his glasses made of flimsy, copper wire.
They bookmarked where he last stopped
reading, and were near his favorite chair.
Grandfather's eyes.

Looking into his face, he gave a distant stare
with the color deteriorated from his cheeks.

Words no longer spoken, he sits in open
spaces, surrounded with strangers who become
friends of commonality. The sounds of loved
ones elate him and bring tears. There

are are no shades of lime or pearl to blanket
grandfather's eyes. The eyes of his soul
continue to see the eyes of ours.
Grandfather's eyes.

Freedom, Let It Ring?

Heed voices of past, present, and future,
Grasp silent, loud struggles of ancestors,
Freedom! Freedom! Freedom!
Let it ring? No!

Wrapped hearts in memories sweat,
Lashes, beatings, lynchings,
Buried blood soiled in the land of this nation,
Freedom! Freedom! Freedom!
Let it ring? No!

People march flooded with triumph,
Shades of color listen, believe, hope,
Equality for one, equality for everyone, equal
rights become human rights,
Freedom! Freedom! Freedom!
Let it ring? No!

Metal chains broken,
Mental chains made,
Trade given, money stolen,

Flesh paid for the land,
Freedom! Freedom! Freedom!
Let it ring? No!

Refusal to move white or colored,
Non-violent sit-ins,
Peaceful protests greeted with countered
resistance,
Years passed,
Inequality cited, reverted,
Freedom! Freedom! Freedom!
Let it ring? No!

God, Moses,
Way maker, friend closer than any other,
Our ancestors followed,
Freedom! Freedom! Freedom!
Let it ring? No!

Justice continuously sounds for the fight for
freedom to move on.
Freedom! Freedom! Freedom!
Let it ring?

The heart decides freedom's ring.

Photo by Daria Nepriakhina

Links

4°

"You cannot measure what hurts, yields joy, and calms the toughest storm, love is immeasurable."

The hospital stay lingered from days into weeks. Eventually, the weeks turned into months and years after leaving Lubbock. The daily spiritual routine in Lubbock heightened my understanding of God's love. I knew God's love, but the awareness of it's power grew stronger and more clear.

The prayer time sparked excitement, love, and hope for James' recovery. Spiritually, I continued to envision James and I standing behind the person on the white horse. We stood dressed in our armor with intense stares and waited for the rider's arm to extend downward to signal a command. A few days or after a full week of praying, we saw the rider's arm extend downward, and I charged forward. I urged James to do the same before realizing the command signaled a battle charge. James and I had no experience with battles, but this one felt real. I refused to lose sight of my brother during the battle, and when the vision ended, James started to recover faster.

The doctors were leery and unconfident in James being able to recover. Initially, when they first delivered the tragic news of his full code, they tried to convince my mother that James had no brain activity, and needed no more tests. They tried to quickly convince my mother and I to stop the machines assisting James' breathing, and they even had the Chief of Neurology advise us on James's condition. I distinctly recall telling him, "Maybe he has not seen anyone recover or live longer than ten years, but I promised in Jesus' name, James would be the first."

The doctors were one-hundred percent certain that James had no activity, but we demanded that they test again. And, to their astonishment, James had brain activity. Inside my heart, I knew James had more time, I knew that God made his power more real to my brother, my mother, and to me.

Brothers

Young boys would fight for the other,
Now, older men, where did the fighting begin
When will it end?

Brothers fight physically for pride in name and
honor,
What honor?
What pride is solved with weapons?

One brother should tell the other when held is
needed,
The other should have a willingness to help
from his heart.
If there is no heart,
There is no life.

A brother should know when the other is ailing.
A brother should know how to lend a healing

hand.

A brother should overlook the bad, and look for the good.

A brother should know the importance and thankfulness of having a brother.

A brother should know how to help, love and

appreciate the other with unity.

What is brotherly love?

Sisters

Good memories arise out of the laughter of
childhood friends,
Cries gathered with joy and loss,
Love remains unwritten, unexplained, and
unconditional between sisters.

Worst seasons can yield the best bonds,
Enemies can become friends,
Years and present moments to time's end,
Sister are dedicated cheerleaders.

Sisters are what God meant for us to be,
A light to shine when darkness peaks.
With loving hearts to endure the stormiest
seas.
We are best friends.
We are sisters.

Hear My Voice

Hear my voice Lord,
Take me by the hand,
Hear my voice Lord,
Give me strength to stand.

Let my heart music sing unto you,
Hear my voice Lord,
In all that you do.

Open my heart,
Shield me from pain,
Open my heart,
Cancel the world of shame.

Take away things and people that don't
represent the love of you,
Open my heart Lord,
And, breathe for me too.

Hear my voice Lord,

With the softness of the wind,
Hear my voice Lord,
Know thy spirit and dwell within.

Mold Me

Mold me my Lord,
Show me thy way,
I don't want to wait to know your grace.

Mold me my Lord,
As time begins to go,
I don't want to wait to see your face.

Mold me my Lord,
Control me my Lord,
Help me increase my faith.

For

In my spirit,
I see no trouble.
(repeat 3 times)

In my spirit,
I see no trouble,
For my Shepherd watches me.

When the storms of life are raging,
I stay in my ship's seat,
For I have a captain who watches me.

I've asked Jesus to carry me,
(repeat 3)
Across the Jordan's river where I am free.

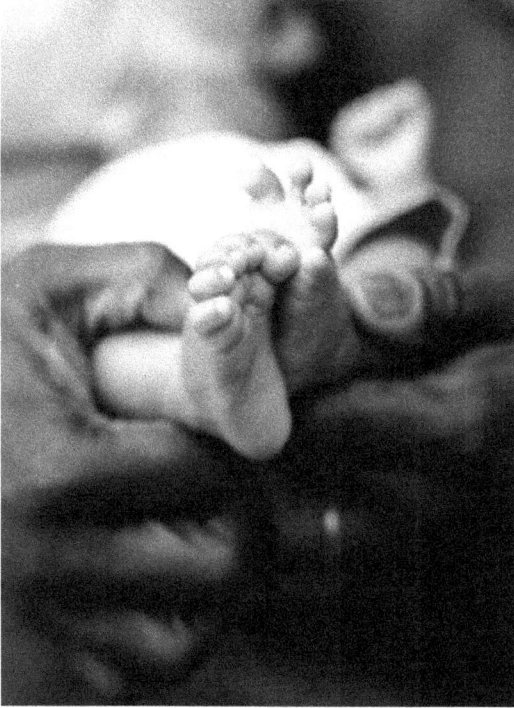

Photo by Jasmine Kossie-jj

Moments Treasured

5°

"Time becomes eternity, a fadeless
entity, but impressions last or are
purposefully dismissed."

The siren emitted no glare or sound, and the
speed of the ambulance was suitable for
transporting James to his destination. We
followed the ambulance and arrived in Austin
after a nine hour drive. Ensuring that James
arrived safely at the rehabilitation facility in
Austin erased any sense of physical tiredness
my mother and I felt.

The rehabilitation facility specialized in brain injuries and had a good reputation in Texas. The facility slightly delayed the formalities of completing the paperwork upon James' arrival, but continued to inform my mother that she needed to provide evidence of James' medical insurance. James' injury gave us a grim, realistic, and quick education in healthcare rights. And, understanding those rights provided an ugly inside perspective on the differences of healthcare in America. The ugliest fact centered on the status quo and its segregation in healthcare.

Politics, corporations, ethnicity, geography, and humanity are the controlling factors in determining quality healthcare. Why humanity? Simple. What human desires anyone to experience pain, or the inability to receive the best opportunity for care? James' medical care and opportunity for recovery became thwarted by insurance companies delaying paper work, losing required documentation, and ineffective filing procedures. The insurances companies, and medical professionals, and the Texas government failed James. They failed to protect and provide for his rights as an American.

James worked as a full-time Captain in corrections, and he prepared for another promotion. He had eighteen semester hours to complete toward a Criminal Justice degree. When James heard the news of becoming a father, he sought stable employment and decided to postpone his degree for later. He worked with friends performing side jobs in construction until he finished his training in corrections. James enjoyed corrections, he excelled in it and earned the respect of colleagues and inmates.

People knew him as a jovial, fair, fun-loving, dedicated, and willing to help individual. James weighed two-hundred and forty pounds, and it was all muscle. As an avid body builder, he could bench press five-hundred pounds and had the trophies to prove it. He maintained a peaceful spirit, disliked confrontation, loved motorcycles and had no criminal background. We were raised in the military, and our father served over twenty-three years as a Lieutenant Colonel, and our mother established a long career in education. James grew up surrounded in diversity, opportunities, and a stable work ethic. James was born an American, he may not have served in the military, but he served as law abiding citizen. The word "American" encompassed a new meaning for James.

The privileges and advantages of being an American are vast and should not be taken for granted. And, anyone who is an American should have equal privileges and privileges should not be based on socioeconomic status and other factors that purposefully cause division. The advantages, great triumphs, and stories are what bind America, but the political, and social issues that segregate America are ugly. And, when the military engages in missions, and wars to preserve America's rights, the status quo continues to preserve an unbalanced, unfair, and biased America. It's as if two magnets are trying to connect opposite ends, and James became stuck in the middle.

During the 2001 political year in Texas, politicians voted for capping medical lawsuits, which meant, if pursuing medical compensation for a medical incident, the compensation would be limited. The justification for placing a cap was based on fear that a shortage of medical professionals would occur. Honestly, if you go into the profession for money, then I think you are not in the profession for helping people. This is not a book of healthcare woes or to disgrace the profession, but it is a book to open the hearts of how political decisions affect everyone, even the lives of the innocent.

While my mother waited the political approval and paper work with James' insurance company, she drove back and forth every day from Killeen to Austin to check on him. Her roundtrip drive totaled two hours pending Austin's traffic, and usually, she drove by herself. She loved being a teacher, and she continued to her work her regular hours, then left work go see James. There were no complaints about her health that she shared, and she did not complain about gas for her car. In her heart, she only cared about James. James stayed in a facility that was unlike the rehabilitation facility we surveyed in Lubbock. This facility appeared organized, clean, and ready to care for Jame's needs, but when James' insurance did not submit his paperwork in a timely fashion, the facility was ready to shove James out the door. And, that's exactly what happened, until the next day.

Our mother stayed one step ahead as much as she could, she knew that since the insurance company and the facility were unwilling to resolve the issue, James needed to have a place to stay, and it needed to be a place closer to her. Eventually, James lived in five facilities and was in and out of the hospital for various reasons or procedures.

One facility caused an injury to James by allowing an infection to develop on his hip. The infection developed due to the lack of required turning and cleaning. The infection bore a hole approximately two inches deep and two inches wide and James had to fight to get his immune system healthy. Another facility subjected James to infections, but when many, elderly, black patients started quickly dying, we moved James to another facility. There are more tales and incidents that have been documented through videos and pictures of the care James received from each facility, however, again, this is not a book of healthcare woes.

Despite the faults of the facilities and the other systems of healthcare, my mother remained a faithful mother. She never asked for or received compensation for gas or supplies for James. And, mostly for ten of the eleven years, she continued to do his laundry, and she continued to provide holiday snacks for his care providers.

Time

Time is gone,
Time is treasured.
Time is to reflect on hope with future dreams.
Time is time.

Two Suns

Two suns each have a horizon,
One in heart,
One the center of the universe.

One seen rising in the east,
And, one risen anywhere it treads.
Pierced light through glass colors are revealed
with one,
Pierced hearts are changed with the other.

Hot, blinding, appearing at certain times to
different parts of the world with temperature
unknown,
A symbol of eternal light without change,
Both have one binding commonality,
Darkness must disappear when light appears.

Time is Now

This day.
This hour.
This minute.
This second.
This breath.
This moment of time is yours.
Take it!

Assurance

Jesus, I know you're here.
Sometimes, I've wondered where.
When the wind blows on my face,
I sense your presence,
I know your grace.
This is a blessed assurance.

Photo by Dylan Gialanella

The Story

6°

"Planning in fear makes life's journey intolerable, and the path of darkness leads to a sure end."

James saw the approaching car and slowed his bike and stopped at the stop sign; he waited for the other driver to make a decision as to whether to turn into the Gentleman's Club or not. James hesitated even while the driver remained indecisive. Then with certainty, James decided to proceed, and the driver did the same. The driver hit James, and upon impact, it caused him to be thrown from his bike, crushing it, and him; he was airlifted to a medical center in Lubbock.

James was a cautious and safe rider. The moment James made the decision to proceed, became the moment that altered life, and the protective gear he wore could not protect James from the unforeseen journey. Donned in his motorcycle gear, James wore red and black leather pants, boots, gloves, a jacket, and a helmet—all part of his gentle persona. Even though Memorial Day 2001 intended to be a day of honoring people who died in service to the United States, this day marked the beginning of an ending of James' life journey.

With the intention to stay home, a friend contacted him to go riding, and he agreed. A short ride around Amarillo, and then back home to enjoy the remainder of the day was his intent. He loved riding his motorcycle, and enjoyed riding since he owned his first motorbike as a teenager, so he had years of riding safely. But, being human did not exclude him from the risk of harm.

I drove mom in her car surpassing the seventy mile per hour speed limit; the odometer read between eighty and ninety. Driving the speed limit was irrelevant, and I sped without consequences, but a highway patrolman stopped me outside of Sweet Water

The citation he issued was better than receiving a ticket after I explained the emergency.

When we arrived in Lubbock, James was in ICU due to the extent of his injuries getting and prepped for surgery. We were allowed to see him, and he displayed a calm, alert, and cheerful attitude; yet, he was in pain. Recounting what happened, James said, "I remember thinking about dad passing and mom living with that tragedy, so I told myself to tuck my head and get into the fetal position."

James' injuries became a roll call of damages that consisted of a broken pelvis, a shattered left wrist caused from holding tightly onto his bikes' handles, a small crack in his shoulder, and torn ligaments in his right knee. No internal organs were damaged, and James had no head injury. The first surgery focused on repairing his broken pelvis and wrist, and it would take hours to complete, so we waited in the ICU family room. Sitting in ICU is daunting, especially when sitting with people who stare, question, and whisper. The ICU waiting room increases grief and hopelessness when surrounded by people who express sadness, anger, and a lack of hope.

A few hours later, James returned from his first successful surgery and was placed back into ICU for monitoring. When I saw him, he mimicked an early replica of a man made of steel. There were approximately one and half inch, iron rods with smaller, stainless steel rods sticking in the sides of his hips and into his midsection. Each iron rod was topped with bolts and screws. James stayed in ICU until he awoke, and a hospital room became available. After his surgery, I remained two more nights to ensure his recovery and to monitor my mother's well-being before flying back home. I needed to go home and help her prepare for a long work absence, and I had to care for my nephew with whom she was raising.

The last day that I saw my brother speaking, alert, and making jokes, I mentioned to my mother to ensure James knew God. The statement about knowing God came out of nowhere, but I felt it, and I urged her to make sure. I took and early flight from Lubbock and left my mother with her car, and knew that it could be awhile before seeing her.

Everyday, she informed me of who visited James, his improvements, and his ability to self-medicate his pain through a pump. The timed morphine pump allowed him to push a button to release the medication; if he pushed the button more than allotted nothing happened. A daily routine of feedback occurred between my mother and I about James's visitors and recovery; it lasted five weeks and seemed promising. James continued to talk with friends, coworkers, and family, while on schedule to have his rods removed from his hips and start rehab after after his knee surgery. No other surgeries were permitted on James until his doctor felt he was stronger from the from first.

One more surgery for repairing his damaged knee was needed before removing the rods from his hips, but the surgery could only happen when James was stronger. Until then, he continued to endure the pain of having his knee in a contraption that automatically extended and stretched it slightly above his head. James hated this; he wanted to start rehab, see his girls, and get back to work. Eventually, he had the knee surgery without complications, until the fifth week since his accident, and I received that call from my mother.

That call was filled with shrieking, crying pain. The pain that I felt in her voice knowingly raised my concern that something was terribly wrong. This is where I begin to end my story, because the beginning is the end. Maybe, our life story should start with the end in mind.

Friends

Friends come and go,
Touching the essence of life,
With barbecues, dominoes, retreats, and
Sunday services,
Friendships are heaven sent from the skies.

Friends do not nag,
And keep you and family in prayer,
Spending time in fellowship,
Giving a peaceful presence in knowing that
they are there.

Friends respect you,
Sharing funny and sad moments on how they
feel,
Friends are present moment gifts,
True, genuine people who keep it real.

Friends pass no judgment,
They simply remind you with olds words far
and above,

That faith, and hope are everything which includes God's love.

Faithful Friends

Unspoken words of wisdom pass in similar
directions,
Weaknesses ever present, but strength prevails
from hidden corners within the soul.

Laughter shared, tears shed, and moments of
respect shown,
Shields of prayer, foundations holding through
time;
Each memory is treasured beyond a limitless
truth.

Faithful friendships ceases not to yield to the
loosening of the bond.

With Gratitude

Money, gifts, and tangible things are costly.
Foundations of friendships are established
through time, wisdom, and willing efforts.

Friendships are short,
Some timeless.
Kindness supersedes in value.
No price or promise,
And, unspoken opportunities to genuinely
serve.

Thank you for the moments you asked, "How
are you?"
Thank you for your ministering smile.
Thank you for inclusion without exclusion.

I've gained opportunities to serve without
expecting anything.

Kindness is priceless, tranquil, and memorable.
With gratitude, "Thank you."

May Peace Exist

Time will reveal the matters of the heart,
This remains true.
That in the darkness you can find light,
And, in your season, God's light shines.

For to be absent in the body,
Is to be present with the Lord.
May tears of your heart be a melody,
May praises you sing bring you peace.

God is the strength that fills your void,
It will encompass you and help ease the pain.
God is with you day to day.

Jesus says, "Walk with me,
Talk with me,
I'll draw near to you."
May there be peace.

Friends are Flowers

Friends are flowers,
Planted and watered for growth,
Friends are flowers uniquely named,
They lose petals,
And, the stems remain the same.

The stems hold bonds together,
Leaves sprout and continue the forever,
Forever is sometimes, and not the original will,
Winds blow scattering seeds to grow and to till.

Friends are flowers you cultivate and each
heart has something to yield,
When you look upon a flower,
You look upon a friend,
And, that is a good lifetime deal.

•Forget- Me-Not – True Love for friends
•Chamomile – Energy in adversity; strength
•Chrysanthemum – Cheerfulness in Adversity
•Water Lily – Eloquence; purity of heart

- Violet – Modesty; faithfulness
- PeriwinkleSincere Friendship, Happy Memories
- Azalea – Temperance

Vision, Mission, Leadership

We are not born to conquer the possible
Time of imparted time and before the existence
of humankind, wisdom breathes

Wisdom knows the direction
Vision creates that path
Mission becomes the compass

Faith turns the impossible into the possible
Leadership is appointed within the soul that
labors with humility for peace.

Photo by Мария Бутырина

Everyday People

70

"Friendships are not measured in the value of their net worth, but in the value of their genuineness to be above the value of things, and in the shared quality, and integrity of character."

Before the life altering surgery James said to our mother, "If anything happens, you fight for me." The tragedy of James' incident may be incomparable to September 9, 2001. Yet, the commonality of anger, grief, and sadness filled my heart, because families had to experience loss, and our nation felt equality through tragedy. There is something ironic about the unfortunate timing of events: James was born on September 8.

On July 7, 2012 a little after midnight, James succumbed to his injuries.

Everyday Is Unfamiliar

Gazing into fields of desert or buildings
uniquely structured,
Across waters and lands of territories
unknown,
Blue, gray, and orange skies fill the horizon,
Everyday is unfamiliar.

Awake with joy and sadness unexpected,
Missing innocent aromas of home,
Voices once annoyed bring true riches to heart,
Everyday is unfamiliar.

Reach within the depth of heart,
Thrust to the forefront ambition and will,
Survive with wisdom and truth,
Carry grace and meekness,
Everyday is an unfamiliar.

Fingers spread and open palms lifted,
Grasp what the eyes may not see,

Memories unfaded and blended through time,
Everyday is unfamiliar.

Loneliness arrives rearing it's ugly head,
Inner strength tested,
Faith is lost by not knowing,
True power comes from the shield within,
Everyday is unfamiliar.

Spoken and hidden to the heart,
Life of the soul is not for the faint,
Abundant living flows from allowed resistance,
Undated miracles heard through centuries,
Sages of wisdom's guide,
Everyday is unfamiliar.

Paths

Individuals journey on paths of destiny,
Shared, crossed, entwined, and paralleled,
Paths are repeated and create directions;
Purposefully paved,
And, purposely different.
Graveled, cobblestone, and paved,
Nothing changes the destination,
Destination changes the path.
Choices change the individual.

Open Windows of Jerusalem

Through the open window I see,
The littlest birds sing,
Praise to the master,
Praise to the Son,
Hallelujah to God.

Through the open windows of Jerusalem,
I hear songs and hymns,
Praise to Jesus the Son of God,
Hallelujah to Him.

Open the windows of Jerusalem,
Let the blessings usher in,
Open the windows of Jerusalem,
Praise to Jesus,
Praise to the Son of God.

Open the windows of Jerusalem,
Hear angels sing,
Open the windows of Jerusalem,
Let the little birds come in.

Open the windows of Jerusalem,
Allow the sun to shine,
Open windows of Jerusalem is where I am
alive.

"In the essence of simplicity is great courage, and a reason to live."
–Kendra

Kendra Turner is a modern day sage with a degree in Social Work and minor in Sociology. Her former education, law enforcement, and technology experience provide a platform for training and speaking.

Kendra is a writer and poet on an unlimited variety of genres. She is self-published and has had other works featured in the *University Press* of Lamar University, *Our Texas Magazine, Spotlight Magazine*, and *Urban Socialites Magazine.*

After battling depression in 2010, Kendra dedicates her life to helping others regain their voice and follow their truth toward happiness. Ms. Turner resides in Atlanta, Georgia.

Meet and stay in touch with Kendra at kendraturner.com